By the Editors of Consumer Guide®

PRACTICAL BOOK OF REMEDIES:

50 Ways to a
BETTER MEMORY

HERMINE HILTON

PUBLICATIONS INTERNATIONAL, LTD.

Hermine Hilton is the director of the Hilton Memory Organization in West Los Angeles and has introduced memory improvement techniques to people of all ages through speeches, programs, and seminars. Hundreds of associations have utilized her expertise in teaching memory skills, including organizations as diverse as NASA, the Department of Justice, Hughes Aircraft, and Exxon. She is a frequent guest on radio programs, and she has made television appearances on the *Today* show, *Late Night with David Letterman,* and CNN. She is the author of *60 Minutes to a Sound Memory* and *The Executive Memory Guide* and is represented by Kessler Management.

Illustration: Darren Thompson

CONTENTS

CONTENTS

YOU DON'T HAVE A TERRIBLE MEMORY!

How many times have you blurted out, "I have a terrible memory," after forgetting someone's name, a phone number, or the directions you were just given? You're not alone. Almost every person *thinks* they have a memory problem. But there's no such thing as a terrible memory—only an untrained one.

Your memory is equal to all the experiences you've already known, all the people—all the places—all the events. It waits to receive all the experiences to come in your future. Memory is the sum total of our lives. And yet many of us never learn how to take control of it. Most people's biggest memory problem is "thinking" they have a problem. And thinking you are alone with your memory problem can make you feel very insecure. The truth is we all suffer from the same "dis-ease." For want of a better term, we'll call it Lack-o-Recall.

We all, on occasion, forget things. Forgetting a name, a number, a note, is normal if you haven't locked it in. If you fail to lock in new information of any kind after seeing it or hearing it, that information can be lost in as little as seven seconds. That's the Seven-Second Syndrome. Lock it or lose it. Usually we fail to lock new information into our memory because we don't know how. This book will show you just how to master your memory and prove to yourself that you have no memory problem.

Sometimes, however, a physical or psychological illness (senile dementia, Alzheimer's disease, hypoglycemia, hematoma, pneumonia, depression, alcoholism, hysteria, and even anxiety) can affect the memory adversely. In these cases it is best to seek out the services of a good physician who is able to prescribe the proper medical care.

However, if you are free of such illnesses and are simply among the many members of the "I forget what I forgot" club, the 50 tips in this book will work for you. Your success with your new ability to recall will probably amaze you. You'll learn how to lock in everything from names to numbers, facts to fictions, spelling to speeches.

1 GET RID OF THOSE BAD HABITS!

Thinking negatively about anything is a bad habit. Your own thoughts about your memory can cause you to forget. Worrying about whether or not you'll remember is a BAD thinking habit that can set your memory up for a fall.

Think of the last time you couldn't recall a name that you knew you should know. When it didn't come to you, maybe you got flustered, tensed up, worried about it—and the harder you tried to remember it, the farther away it seemed to slip. Maybe this wasn't the first time it happened. If so, you may have built up an anxiety about it and convinced yourself you just *don't* remember names. When you meet new people, instead of trying to capture their names, perhaps you give up before you even begin. What a shame.

Worrying about whether you will forget only makes matters worse.

Worrying about anything sends the wrong message to your mind. You might as well send it a direct order to forget. Even though you're not consciously aware of it, your subconscious mechanically collects everything you're seeing, hearing, feeling, or even thinking about. It will collect a message saying you can't remember names. Since you have no control over your subconscious, you never know when these negative thoughts will come back to haunt you.

Other negative habits that promote forgetting stem from fear that your memory will embarrass you, ignorance of how to improve your memory, and uneasiness about making changes. Memory improvement involves learning new habits. Many people harbor objections to the pain of having to learn anything new. ("But—I haven't the time." "But—is it really necessary?" "But—it might not be that easy.") Don't be preset to forget. Don't be the last to try anything new. A new method could be a sure cure for something that doesn't work well. Not wanting to try it is not merely a bad habit. It is costly and a waste of good energy. Don't let your objections stop you from enjoying future benefits. You can rid yourself of bad memory habits by understanding how your memory works. Once you learn how your memory works, then you can work your memory.

STOP JOKING ABOUT YOUR MEMORY.

"My brain's taken a vacation." "I couldn't remember a thing to save my soul." "My memory's like a sieve with a hole in it." Does this sound familiar? When you forget something, is it easier to toss it off as a joke than to seek an intelligent remedy for your lapse?

Well, all these "in one ear and out the other" lines should be stricken from your thoughts. All the jokes in the world won't help your memory. They only make it worse.

Everything you say or think drops into the storehouse of the subconscious mind. Even though *you* know you are joking, the subconscious mind takes everything literally. You've sent your subconscious a directive that sooner or later may become a self-fulfilling prophesy.

If you keep on joking about your bad memory, don't be surprised when you go to introduce your wife to your boss and can't remember her name. That could be just the moment when your subconscious memory—over which you have no control—decides to send you a reminder of the recorded message you have been so readily and jokingly sending to yourself.

Put an end to the "in one ear and out the other" jokes!

3 STOP—LOOK—AND LISTEN.

The first step toward improving your memory is to learn to focus on the people and things around you. To focus means to pay attention. To improve your memory, pay attention by making yourself aware of what you want to remember. This is called creating original awareness. It is a necessary step that sets the scene and gets us prepared to collect new information.

Have you ever left someone's house and not been able to recall a single detail of its decor? Have you ever conversed with someone at length and yet had no idea, after their departure, what they had been talking about? Have you ever walked or jogged around the same area over a period of time and yet been unable to name the streets? The reason is not that you have a poor memory. The reason is you did not create original awareness. You did not bother to focus on the information.

Focusing involves three basic combined actions: seeing and hearing (paying attention), looking and listening (thinking about what is seen or heard), and comprehending and digesting (putting it all together). All three start with taking an interest in what goes on around you.

Don't run right past the things you want to remember! Create original awareness by focusing on them.

SWITCH ON YOUR CONSCIOUS MIND.

4

The human memory is often referred to as the greatest computer in the universe. But in order to work it, you must first switch it on. Turning on the power of your memory means switching on the power of your conscious mind—the controlled, awake, and attentive memory—rather than relying on your mechanical memory (the subconscious, automatic memory).

If we don't make a conscious effort to focus on new information, it goes into our mechanical or subconscious memory. Even though we've seen or heard the information, we often can't access or recall it. This is because the eye and the ear do not do the remembering. The eye does the seeing and the ear does the hearing, but only the mind does the remembering. The information goes "in one ear and out the other"—we can't recall it because we merely heard it; we didn't learn it. To improve our memories, we need to consciously wake up our minds to what we are seeing or hearing.

DON'T BLAME FORGETFULNESS ON YOUR AGE.

5

How many times have you heard that as the years go, so goes the memory? How often does grandma say, "My memory's not as good as it used to be"—and then just allows herself to forget? But current scientific studies show that barring illness to the brain, the adverse effect your age has on your memory ability is a myth. In fact, the opposite is true. Memory, it has now been found, is one of the few things that can actually improve with age. Because the mind is a connecting machine ("and that reminds me . . ."), the older we get, the more experiences and knowledge we have stored away to connect with. Keep active mentally and physically. A stimulated brain at any age will continue to sprout connections. All we have to do is learn how to best activate our connecting machine. And this book can be your guide.

If you should fail to recall some one thing, don't use your age as an excuse. That excuse doesn't hold water anymore. And you shouldn't let an idea that doesn't hold water anymore drown you.

6   FOLLOW THE AGELESS LEADERS.

Nobody (of any age) grows old until they lose enthusiasm for living and stop making memories. Exchange your negatives for positives—focus on these role models. They couldn't have succeeded as they did without utilizing their memories throughout their lives.

- Cornelius Vanderbilt was older than the present mandatory retirement age when he consolidated his railroad empire and built one of the world's most immense fortunes.
- Fritz Kreisler played his violin as well at 74 as he ever did.
- Pablo Casals at 88 was still giving cello concerts.
- Georges Clemenceau was 76 when he became premier of France to lead his country to victory in World War I. He presided over the Paris Peace Conference, which drew up the Treaty of Versailles, at the age of 78.
  - Mary Baker Eddy was directing the Christian Science Church at 89.
  - Giuseppe Verdi wrote one of his finest operas, *Falstaff,* when he was 80 years old.
  - Victor Hugo produced *Les Miserables* when he was 60 and was still writing poetry in his 80s.
  - Titian painted his "Pieta" at 85.
  - Goethe finished Part II of *Faust* when he was over 80.
  - George Bernard Shaw was still writing plays in his 90s.
  - Andrew Mellon, the financier and industrialist, served as Secretary of the Treasury until he was 76, and he became ambassador to Britain after that.
  - Coco Chanel was head of a fashion design firm at 85.
  - Eleanor Roosevelt was a delegate to the United Nations and an outspoken advocate of human rights up to the time of her death at 78.
- Immanuel Kant never said "can't," and he wrote some of his greatest philosophical works after he was 70.
- Leopold Stokowski formed and led the American Symphony Orchestra in New York when he was 80.

Keep your vitality and interest in life, and you'll take a big step in retaining your memory.

Thomas Alva Edison continued to work into his 80s.

MAKE A "FOCUS ON PEOPLE" CHART.

7

We want the people we meet and work with to feel positive about us. To do that, we must help them to feel positive about themselves as well. This means taking a personal interest in who they are and what they are about. We must give them our focus from the first sound of their names.

A fun way to create original awareness of people is to make a "Focus on People" chart. This technique is especially good for doctors, dentists, lawyers, accountants, and other professionals who want to remember the many people they meet throughout the day.

The "Focus on People" chart lists each appointment hour of the day. The person being focused on in that time slot resides in a special box resembling a house. Spaces in each "house" include the person's name, what their name makes you think of, their general appearance, any outstanding feature, their occupation, spouse's name, children's names, hobbies, and all the information you should be focusing on in order for you to know them. You can find out this information simply by asking for it. People usually like sharing and appreciate your caring. Review the chart from time to time, and the information entered there will soon be part of your memory. All it takes is a little FOCUS!

A professional needs to remember details about many people.

8

DON'T DEPEND ON ROTE MEMORY.

The dictionary defines rote memory as "mindless repetition with little or no intelligence or understanding involved." And without understanding there is no value. In school we were usually told *what* to learn but not *how* to learn it. So if we studied by rote, moving our eyes over pages and pages of material—often heedless of its meaning—we were lucky if some of it stuck. And if it did, it probably didn't stick for long. You may recall a cram session the night before a big exam. You probably still felt insecure going into the exam, and by now you probably remember very little of what you crammed. There's the proof that rote memorizing produces very little intelligent remembering.

Repetition doesn't necessarily produce genuine learning. How many times have you seen a penny? Can you say for sure which way Lincoln is facing? Do you know what kind of numerals are on your wristwatch— Roman or Arabic? Merely repeating, seeing, or hearing something over and over again doesn't guarantee you can recall it.

You often hear that the only thing you have to do to remember something is to repeat it often enough. This misconception is a mindless idea. Don't depend on it! Repetition is not enough. You must focus on what you want to remember and learn it.

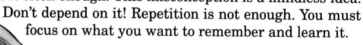

Does Lincoln face right . . . or does he face left?

USE MNEMONICS.

9

The science of memory training is called mnemonics. A mnemonic is a mental thought connector. Pronounced *ne-MAH-nik* (the first *m* is silent), it comes from the Greek word meaning "of the mind." The Greek goddess Mnemosyne ruled the memory in the ancient Hellenic world, and today she might reign over the intricate workings of the computer's memory. All computer programs use mnemonic codes to store and retrieve information. And so does the human mind, which, as we know, invented the computer in the first place.

Mnemonic learning is the exact opposite of rote learning (which isn't real learning at all). Mnemonic techniques employ the skill of consciously gathering new memory (information) and connecting it to prior memory (knowledge) for easy recall. If you meet someone named Webster, it might make you think of Webster's dictionary. You've now connected something new (the person's name) with something known. The connection itself is the mnemonic.

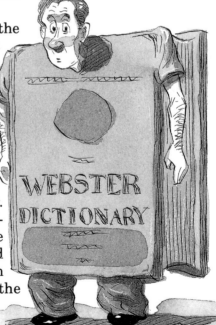

Connect Mr. Webster to the dictionary.

Don't feel alone if you didn't know that Mr. Lincoln was facing to the right on the penny, or you couldn't say for sure, without looking, what kind of numerals are on your watch, or you forgot the first person you were introduced to today by the time you met the second. And don't blame it on a faulty memory, either. You merely need to learn how to learn.

We now know that our eyes and ears cannot by themselves do the remembering. If we want to remember something, we must make a conscious mental connection between what the eye is seeing or the ear is hearing and something the mind already knows.

If you're a trivia player and want to lock in that profile of Mr. Lincoln's, connect his right profile with the idea that the president always tried to do "right" by the people. Your physical eye and ear are now sending a message to your "mind's ear," which is thought. And that's what mnemonics is all about. By making the conscious connection from new intelligence to known intelligence, you are pressing the REMEMBER button in your mind.

10 GET RID OF THE SEVEN-SECOND SYNDROME.

"Forgetting" really means never "getting" it in the first place. And you can't "forget" what you never "got." The Seven-Second Syndrome means that within seven seconds of seeing or hearing something, you can lose it. That happens when your mind doesn't focus on it and lets your eyes or ears go it alone.

Ever gotten a telephone number from the information operator, dialed it and heard a busy signal, and then couldn't recall the number when you went to redial it? Ever been introduced to someone and by the time you finished saying hello, their name was a blank? Both cases of the Seven-Second Syndrome. Your machine just wasn't connected. Banish the Seven-Second Syndrome by focusing your mind on the information you want to remember.

11 BE PREPARED TO REMEMBER.

The basic formula for remembering anything involves three steps:
1. COLLECTING the information,
2. CONNECTING WITH the information, and
3. RECOLLECTING the information.
This is an important 1-2-3 formula to keep in mind.

We all desire to gather information for either short-term needs or long-term recall. For small bits of information—usually for short-term holds, say until we can get to a pencil and paper—we can learn simple mnemonic techniques. These include acronyms, acrostics, rhyming, and the like.

You can also gather larger amounts of information and file it in the mind for long-term availability. For this you can use a more permanent method—a mental file from which you can extract information in any sequence.

If you learn how to use mnemonics, you will be prepared to remember. You will avoid the Seven-Second Syndrome. Everyone can do it—regardless of age or IQ. Just as everyone's arms and legs bend in the same direction, memory for everyone works according to the same formula.

INVENT AN ACRONYM.

12

Phrases and titles are often difficult to remember without mnemonic help. An acronym is a word formed from the first letters of the words that make up a phrase. Some acronyms reproduce the meaning of the words they stand for. MADD stands for Mothers Against Drunk Driving. The Group Against Smog and Pollution cleverly uses the acronym GASP to represent its organization.

Acronyms are not necessarily actual words that relate to what they stand for. But the good ones can become just as memorable in time. You're familiar with ASAP (As Soon As Possible) and SASE (Self-Addressed Stamped Envelope). Some acronyms have become words—SCUBA stands for Self-Contained Underwater Breathing Apparatus.

Creating an acronym from the initials of an entire phrase makes the phrase easy to remember, for by recalling the single word you can recall all the parts. The next time you have a tricky phrase or title you'd like to remember, try inventing an acronym.

Trying to keep track of the names of your sister's four rambunctious toddlers Richard, Roberta, Arthur, and Olga? Make up an acronym. You can spell ROAR—R for Richard, O for Olga, A for Arthur, and another R for Roberta—and you can imagine your sister "roaring" at them to quiet down.

Or let's say you want to remember the order in which your car pool takes turns driving to work. The names are Eaton, Simpson, Grant, and Larson. You can create the acronym LEGS, which is easy to remember— if you carpool, you won't use your LEGS for walking.

13 CREATE AN ACROSTIC.

An acrostic is an initialing strategy similar to an acronym. Instead of having the letters make up a word, though, the letters stand for the words in a sentence. If you ever took music lessons, you probably learned the sentence "Every Good Boy Does Fine"—the first letters of each word stand for the musical notes on the lines of the staff, E, G, B, D, and F.

Here's another example. If you wanted to remember the names of the planets in our solar system in their right order, you could do so with the thought: "My Very Earthy Mother Just Served Us Nine Pizzas!"

My = Mercury

Very = Venus

Earthy = Earth

Mother = Mars

Just = Jupiter

Served = Saturn

Us = Uranus

Nine = Neptune

Pizzas = Pluto

Want to remember to return phone calls to Harry, Ike, Elsie, Sam, and Unger? Why not try "How Is Everything Shaping Up?" If you want to remember the order of your exams in physics, French, math, and English, try "Preparing For My Education!"

TRY RHYTHM AND RHYMING.

14

Did you ever get yourself into hot water because you forgot an appointment, someone's birthday, or an anniversary? Creating and reciting a rhyme could save you from this kind of predicament. Rhythm and rhyme have always been very helpful in remembering. Because of a rhyme, you can probably right now give the exact year Columbus sailed the ocean blue. How do you remember which months have 30 days? With the rhyme:

Thirty days hath September,
April, June, and November.

Think how many television commercials you remember because the product message is delivered with rhythm and rhyme.

Here are some ideas to use rhythm and rhyme for your own needs.

For an anniversary:

Our honeymoon was first of June
On August 4, we shut the door

For a birthday:

May the 12th, 1907, Grandma Lena came from heaven
Baby beckoned March the 2nd

A letter due out:

Send a word by the 3rd

A court date:

December 8—don't be late for the magistrate

For names:

Dance with Lance; Schuster's a rooster; Mitch is rich
The cook Leonetti makes spaghetti
Pierre Hoctor is my doctor
Mrs. Blair has got red hair

By the way, just in case you were absent that day:

In fourteen hundred and ninety-two,
Columbus sailed the ocean blue.

MAKE A MENTAL MEMO.

HINT

If you need to remember to call someone, or do something, at a specific time, set the alarm. If your wristwatch has an alarm, use it.

Remembering to do the many small things in life can sometimes be very important. Forgetting to take your medicine, for example, could have serious consequences.

We can make mental memos to remember these things. A mental memo is a thought prompter set in your mind. The old "string around the finger" routine is an example of a mental memo. It's an old joke that you will look at the string and wonder why it's there. That won't happen if you take an interest in doing whatever it is you need to do and pay conscious attention to why you're tying the string around your finger. Today, however, it's handier to use a rubber band.

Here's another mental memo: If you want to remember to take your vitamins in the morning, leave the vitamin bottle upside down on the bathroom sink. Upon seeing it in the morning when you go to brush your teeth, the upside-down bottle will remind you.

Another good memory jogger is to link something that you want to remember with an item you are sure to see. If you want to cash a check at the bank, you could put the check on top of your wallet or purse. You'll surely remember to take it with you on your way out.

If the TV weatherman says rain is expected, hook an umbrella over the knob of the front door.

You'll remember to take with you a letter you want to mail by putting it underneath your car keys. When you go out, you can drive yourself right to a mailbox.

To remember to buy theater tickets on your way back from lunch, make a mental memo to pay two bills at lunch—one for lunch and one for the theater tickets. Later, when you actually pay the lunch bill, you'll be reminded to stop at the theater.

Get into the habit of making mental memos to remember the things you have to do. Soon remembering to do them will become a habit.

PRACTICE MENTAL FILING.

If you keep a personal organizer or notebook listing all the things you need to do each day, get in the habit of looking at it first thing each morning and several times during the day, checking off all your chores as you complete them.

But sometimes you need to remember things that occur to you when you can't write them down. The solution is to mentally file them.

It's easy, and you can start right now. Let's use as an example a number of things that anyone might have to do today: see the eye doctor, buy a gift, pay your credit card bill, order stationery, fix the car radio, call the school principal, and buy vitamins. We'll call these our TTDTs (Things To Do Today).

If each of us had a permanent mental filing system, we could use it for a mnemonic connection every time we got a new piece of information. The simplest of mnemonic head-start techniques for filing things mentally is to make a list of numbered word cues. These cues are words that rhyme with the numbers 1 through 7.

1 = SUN

2 = SHOE

3 = FEE

4 = DOOR

5 = DRIVE

6 = TRICKS

7 = HEAVEN

Make a mental picture of each word in your mind. Mentally hear the rhyme. Run through the cues until you're sure you've locked them in. Test yourself.

Once your cues are set in your mind, file in your Things To Do Today by making a connecting thought from each cue to each TTDT.

Rhyme cue	Connecting thought
1. Sun	My **eye doctor** may prescribe **sun**glasses.
2. Shoe	I'll look for a **gift** in the **shoe** department.
3. Fee	If I don't **pay the bill** they'll raise the **fee.**
4. Door	I'll have the **stationery** delivered to my **door.**
5. Drive	I'll fix the **car radio** so I can enjoy the **drive.**
6. Tricks	Will the **principal** say the kids are up to some **tricks?**
7. Heaven	Do they sell **vitamins** in **heaven?**

Now recall your word cues and let the rhyming words tick off your TTDTs. Once you have your TTDTs firmly in mind, you can relax and go about your day knowing your tasks are filed. Check them off as you do them. Use the same rhyming word cues again tomorrow for new TTDTs. Add more rhyme cues if you need more numbers on your list.

With a little practice, you'll find it easy to remember your TTDTs. When you mentally check them off, by the end of each day you'll have TCOB—Taken Care Of Business!

BRING HOME THE BACON WITH A MNEMONIC SHOPPING LIST.

17

You can apply mnemonic techniques to your lists of things to buy. If you're going to the drugstore and need to pick up dental floss, nasal spray, hair conditioner, and air freshener, you could make up an acronym:

Hair conditioner - **H**

Air freshener - **A**

Nasal spray - **N**

Dental floss - **D**

Then, when you leave the drugstore, all the things you need will be right in your HAND.

If you're going to the market to buy things for a party, your list might include oysters, caviar, Dom Perignon champagne, shrimp, Swedish meatballs, and peppers. You could create an acrostic sentence: "Please, mother, do come over soon."

Please - **P**eppers

Mother - **M**eatballs (Swedish)

Do - **D**om Perignon

Come - **C**aviar

Over - **O**ysters

Soon - **S**hrimp

On your way home from the market, you need to pick up a cake you ordered at the bakery. Put a birthday candle in your wallet, and when you pay for your purchases at the market, the candle will remind you to stop at the bakery. (Or simply put in a note saying "CAKE" if you can't find a candle.)

Try a little rhythm and rhyming to lock in these staples:
"Cereal, milk, eggs, and bread—
That should keep the kids well fed."
Or practice a little mental filing, using the rhyme word cues, to bring home the bacon.
Here's our list:

bacon	wine
candy	steak
flowers	hot dogs
ice cream	oranges
apples	napkins

Since we have ten items, we'll add three more rhyme cues:

  8 = PLATE
  9 = SIGN
10 = HEN

Set the shopping list items into your mental file in any order that best fits each rhyme cue.

Rhyme cue	Item	Thought connector
1. Sun	oranges	Florida **oranges** grow in the **sun.**
2. Shoe	steak	Hope the **steak** isn't tough as **shoe** leather.
3. Fee	wine	There's a tax (**fee**) on **wine.**
4. Door	flowers	Leave the **flowers** at the **door.**
5. Drive	hot dogs	We'll eat **hot dogs** on the **drive.**
6. Tricks	candy	**Trick** or treat for **candy** on Halloween.
7. Heaven	ice cream	This **ice cream** is **heavenly.**
8. Plate	napkins	Put **napkins** on each **plate.**
9. Sign	apples	**Apple Annie** carried a **sign.**
10. Hen	bacon	The **hen** made friends with the **pig.**

DEVELOP EAR-MINDEDNESS.

Even though the initial impact of seeing is said to be much stronger than that of any other sense, what we see is often not slated for longevity in the mind. The mind's ear is a much more important tool than the mind's eye. In fact, an auditory message to the mind's ear can bring about a visual image en route. For example, if someone tells you *not* to visualize a pink elephant, chances are you're already seeing one.

Even when names, numbers, and facts are seen printed on a card or written on a page, the letters and numbers don't really stimulate the mind's eye. But hearing those same names, numbers, and facts wakes up our memory machine. That is why the best approach to getting into the mnemonic habit is to become more ear-minded. Things register in our memory through our five senses. In most cases, seeing and hearing are the most predominant senses. People who feel they remember best what they see may think of themselves as eye-minded. People who remember best what they hear are ear-minded. A motor-minded person obtains memories through the remaining senses of touch, taste, and smell.

Most of us possess each of the three qualities to some degree. No person is 100 percent eye-, ear-, or motor-minded, not even the person who has a photographic memory. We all have the ability to develop and improve any or all of these senses. To make remembering a habit, try to develop your ear-mindedness by consciously listening more to everything you hear.

You'll be surprised how much more interesting, even entertaining, such things as names can be when you lend an ear. Start by noticing every name you hear. Pay attention to the names of the news people on television, street names, company names, the names of radio hosts and their guests, authors' names, the names of their books and publishers, musicians' names and the names of their instruments, actors' names and the characters they portray, or any names that come within hearing distance.

This added aural attention will increase and develop your ear-mindedness. It will begin to make the unfamiliar familiar. Hearing anything the second time around increases recognition and helps us to connect mentally with new information. And that's what our memory—our connecting machine—is all about.

19 HIT THE "SAVE" KEY.

As many of us learned the hard way, after entering information into a computer, you have to press the SAVE key, or all of that information—or memory—is literally erased when the computer is turned off. It is as though it was never processed at all. Humans experience the same phenomenon with memory. If we see or hear information that we don't consciously wire into our minds, that information becomes inaccessible.

In order to make the information retrievable, we first have to run it by our mind's ear. The physical ear does the hearing, but it's the mind's ear that does the listening. It is the mind's ear that can think about what you hear and connect with it.

Get into the habit of connecting with information by doing consciously what the mind cannot do unconsciously. Upon hearing anything that you want to remember, hit the SAVE key on your own mental computer. Here's how to do that. The moment you hear or see a name, number, fact, or piece of information that could be of value to you, immediately ask yourself this seven-word question: "What does this make me think of?" The momentary thought that this requires focuses your mind on the information. It's just like pressing a SAVE key, but most people ignore this basic step. And yet hitting the SAVE key is the most vital step in taking control of your memory.

WHAT DOES THIS MAKE ME THINK OF?

To remember, be like "The Thinker"—as soon as you hear something you want to remember, ask yourself this important question.

SEARCH FOR THE "SONIKS."

What are Soniks? The word SONIK is invented from *sonic* (having to do with sound and the speed of sound) and pertains to the sound of words and what they remind you of. A Sonik memory uses the sounds of the names of things to capture information in the quickest possible way.

Most names and terms sound like or somehow resemble other names and terms. And noting this similarity helps us to connect with and lock in new information. That's why when we ask ourselves, "What does this make me think of?" we will compare what we are hearing to something we've heard before. We are hitting the SAVE key by searching for the Soniks. We are searching for something familiar to relate the new information to. Becoming more ear-minded makes sounds more familiar to us, and that familiarity breeds recognition, which helps to lock in knowledge.

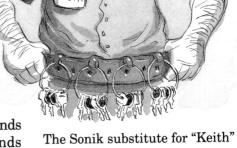

One of the best places to practice looking for Soniks is in names. Names that give you meaning are true Soniks. Some true Sonik names are Ford, Carpenter, Rivers, Foster, Taylor, and Goldberg. (Remember, only the sound counts, so spelling doesn't matter.)

Names that you give meaning to are called Sonik substitutes. Some Sonik substitutes would be Robert (sounds like "robber"), Hotchkiss (sounds like "hot kiss"), Guttman (sounds like "good man"), and Keith (sounds like "keys").

The Sonik substitute for "Keith" is "keys."

You can also find Soniks and Sonik substitutions in many numerals.

1 is the same as "won,"
3 sounds like "free,"
4 is the same as "fore,"
8 is the same as "ate."

Soniks can be found in most things you hear if you take the time to listen. Develop your Sonik memory and help yourself hit the SAVE key!

21 LOOK FOR MATHEMATICAL PATTERNS.

Some people have a knack for remembering numbers, but for many of us, numbers are the hardest things to remember. The more numbers that get thrown at us, the more confusing they become. They all look alike, and they don't appeal to any of our five senses. In a nutshell, they are boring.

To latch onto numbers, switch on your conscious and search for the mathematical patterns within them. Large numbers are made up of individual digits. Often the combination of digits can remind us of something we can relate to. The number 654 represents a natural descending sequence, whereas 234 is a natural progression. You can remember 729 by thinking that 7 + 2 = 9. The number 248 is another natural progression—each digit is double the preceding one. The number 24816 works the same way if you consider the last two digits as a unit. Square numbers are easy to spot. The number 981 reminds us that 9 is the square root of 81 ($9 \times 9 = 81$).

It's easier to grasp longer numbers by splitting them into parts. When the operator shoots a telephone number at you, think of the last four digits as double-digit numbers. If you want to remember 769-3259, you'd probably find it easier to remember 32 and 59 than the 3 and 2 and 5 and 9. Two numbers are always easier to remember than four, and you'll be less likely to transpose them.

Give numbers a good arithmetical looking-over when trying to commit them to memory. Finding any combination, progression, or mathematical relationship will make numbers much easier to remember.

When the operator gives you a phone number, break it into parts.

GIVE DIGITS MEANING.

22

Not every number has a mathematical pattern or stimulates the imagination. Since numbers do not convey ideas or create pictures for the mind to visualize, we must do it for them. We do it by finding the Soniks in numbers, mentally substituting thought cues for digits. We call these Numerik cues.

Simple Numeriks are for recalling isolated numbers (telephone numbers, addresses, safe-deposit box numbers, and the like). The more complex Master Numerik Alphabet (see page 30) is used for longer numbers, lists of numbers, and numbers that must be remembered in a particular order. You already have some ready-made Numerik connectors to certain digits, although you may not have thought about them in this way. Some numbers are personally significant—birthdays, anniversaries, number of children, or their ages. Others are famous numbers—5 is a nickel, 7 is lucky, 13 unlucky, 16 sweet. Some are famous dates—1776, 1492, 1865, 1941—depending on how well you liked history. Some are used in brand names—57 Varieties, 7/11 stores. Many digits stick in your mind from nursery rhymes and stories you learned in childhood—3 Little Pigs, 10 Little Indians. When you hit the SAVE key, any of these Numerik cues may pop up.

Another way to make numbers easier to collect is to think of them as dollars and cents. You could remember 1589 by translating it to $15.89, and 42199 might be $421.99. Money is always easier to remember than meaningless digits.

Notice all the Sonik connectors you can relate to in the numbers you see and hear. And using any combination of these simple Numerik techniques, you'll be on your way to giving digits meaning.

23

CREATE NUMERIK REMINDERS FOR PHONE NUMBERS AND ADDRESSES.

Here's a list of simple Numerik cues from 1 to 25 to use as needed, along with the phonetic sounds of the digits and your own Sonik connectors.

1 = Number One (that's you)
2 = Two to Tango
3 = Three Musketeers
4 = Four-leaf clover
5 = Five cents (a nickel)
6 = Six-shooter
7 = Lucky seven
8 = Eight ball
9 = Cloud nine
10 = Ten Little Indians
11 = A payoff number (dice game)
12 = A dozen
13 = Unlucky number
14 = Valentine's Day
15 = Income tax day
16 = Sweet 16
17 = *Seventeen* magazine
18 = Draft age
19 = Last of teen years

20 = 20/20 vision

21 = Blackjack (a card game)

22 = Tutu (a ballet costume)

23 = Rhymes with "plenty free"

24 = Hours in a day

25 = A quarter (25 cents)

Now, thinking Numerikally, let's put the following numbers in your mental telephone/address book.

Addresses and apartment or suite numbers:

822	I **ate too too** much!
4050	Who cares if you're **40** or **50?**
1031, #22	On **Halloween** I'll wear a **tutu.**
517, #12	If it only costs a **nickel** for *Seventeen* magazine, I'll take a **dozen.**

Telephone numbers:

830-1225	I woke up at **8:30** on **Christmas.**
214-1365	**Valentine's Day** comes **once** a **year.**
550-1969	I gave **$550** to the **first man on the moon.**
415-1018	On **income tax day,** the **Ten Little Indians** were **drafted.**

Why not work out a Numerik reminder for your own address and telephone number? The next time someone asks you for it, they won't even have to write it down.

24 STUDY THE MASTER NUMERIK ALPHABET.

If you really want to get serious and create a master mental file, memorize the Master Numerik Alphabet. Based on a principle first discovered in the 18th century, it assigns consonant sounds to each of the ten single digits. You can translate each digit of a number into its consonant sounds and then insert vowels between the consonants to create words. The words will be easier for you to remember than the number.

Here's the Master Numerik Alphabet:

Number	Sound	Reminder cue
1	T or D or Th	The **Number 1** team made a **TouchD**own.
2	N	A written **N** has **2** loops.
3	M	A written **M** has **3** loops.
4	R	It's the **4**th letter in the word fou**R**.
5	L	Roman numeral for **50**.
6	Sh, Ch, J, or soft G	Add up **6** letter symbols in **6**th group.
7	K, hard C, Q, or hard G	To write a capital **K,** you start with a **7.**
8	F or V	Mr. **F**ord made a **V8** engine.
9	P or B	**P** is **9** backward, and **B** is a pregnant **P**.
0	Z, S, or soft C	**Z**ero (**0**) is spelled with a **Z**, and **S** and **C** and **Z** are all sibilantly similar.

You'll notice some digits have more than one consonant option, yet each option imparts the same or a very similar phonetic sound. The vowels A,

E, I, O, and U have no numerical value in this alphabet, nor do silent letters. Similarly, the sounds made by the letters that spell the word WHY—the W, the H, and the Y—have no value.

The entire focus of this alphabet is on the sound that the consonant letters are making—not the letters themselves.

By translating numbers into phonetic sounds, we can use those sounds to form words and phrases that are more memorable than the numbers. Then, by recollecting that word or phrase, we can recall the number.

The number 48 would have the two consonant sounds R and F. It could be translated to the word ROUGH—spelling doesn't matter; it's the sound that counts. The number 48 could also translate to RAVE, RIFF, ROVE, ROOF, ARRIVE.

The word PHASE, which has the consonant sounds of an F and a Z, could be used to remember the number 80. You could also use VOICE, VASE, FUSE, or FACE.

The G and H are silent in the word NIGHT, so it has only the consonant sounds of an N and a T. It can be used to remember the number 21. Or you could use NET, NUT, ANT, KNIGHT, and even HAND and HOUND (remember the H sound has no value).

It may seem hard to get used to, but the Master Numerik Alphabet is well worth the trouble of memorizing and studying. With it, you can create not just words, but long phrases to translate and remember those long numbers like social security numbers and credit card numbers.

25

PRACTICE USING THE MASTER NUMERIK ALPHABET.

It just takes a little imagination to translate numbers to words and phrases. Here are some examples. Check the letter sounds in these phrases with your Master Alphabet to understand just how it works.

LOCK COMBINATION 31-43-25

3	1	4	3	2	5
M	T	R	M	N	L
My	Te	R	Mi	Na	L

My Terminal

PHONE NUMBER 732-7151

7	3	2	7	1	5	1
C	M	N	C	T	L	D
Co	Mmu	Ni	Ca	Te	aLl	Day

Communicate All Day

BANK ACCOUNT 849-84507-6

8	4	9	8	4	5	0	7	6
F	R	B	V	R	L	S	C	SH
Fo	R	Be	Ve	R	Ly'	S	Ca	SH

For Beverly's Cash

PASSPORT 034131485

0	3	4	1	3	1	4	8	5
S	M	R	T	M	T	R	V	L
Su	Mme	R	Ti	Me	T	Ra	Ve	L

Summertime Travel

SOCIAL SECURITY 941-71-0950

9	4	1	7	1	0	9	5	0
P	R	T	C	T	S	P	L	S
P	Ro	Te	C	T	uS	P	Lea	Se

Protect Us Please

CREDIT CARD 5105-9841-2770-9208

5	1	0	5	9	8	4	1	2	7	70	9	2	0	8
L	T	S	aL	B	V	R	T	N	G	X	P	N	S	V
Le	T	uS	aLl	Buy	eVe	Ry	Thi	N	G	eX	Pe	N	Si	Ve

Let Us All Buy Everything Expensive

Notice that the X sound is a combination of two sounds, K and S, so it translates as 70.

CREDIT CARD 1215-1220-4741-1741

1	2	1	5	1	2	2	0	4	7	4	1	1	7	4	1
D	N	T	L	T	N	N	S	R	C	R	D	T	C	R	D
Do	N'	T	Le	T	aNy	oNe	uSe	youR	C	Re	Di	T	Ca	R	D

Don't Let Anyone Use Your Credit Card

Start practicing right now by flipping through your address book and creating phrases for the phone numbers you use most frequently. Write them right into your address book and say them to yourself whenever you dial them. Eventually the phrase will become part of your memory—and the address book will be history.

26 PRACTICE CONNECTING WITH SIMPLE FACTS.

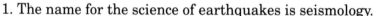

Have you ever been to a gathering where someone suggests a game of trivia? You feel you should know the answers, but you just can't come up with them. Everyone needs to remember at least a few simple facts. Practice hitting your SAVE key and mentally connecting with new facts.

Here are some isolated pieces of information. As you read each one, lock it in by asking yourself, "What does this make me think of?"

1. The name for the science of earthquakes is seismology.
2. The 29th president of the United States was Harding.
3. The four states in the United States that connect at their corners are Utah, Colorado, Arizona, and New Mexico.
4. Acrophobia is a fear of heights.
5. Benjamin Franklin invented bifocals.
6. The largest collection of dinosaurs in the United States is in Pittsburgh.
7. On a ship, port is left and starboard is right.
8. In the lower brain, the seat of memory is the hippocampus, which directs the thalamus to file memories.

Here are some mnemonic connections that come to mind.

1. What is the **size** of the **earthquake?** (From the sound of *seismology.*)
2. The year **'29** was a **hard** year.
3. The acronym **UCAN** covers all their initials, and **U-CAN** step on the place that connects them.
4. The **acrobat** goes to great **heights.**
5. **B.F.** invented **B-F.**
6. Lots of **dinosaurs** are in the **Pits.**
7. Aim **right** for the **stars** and you won't be **left** back at the **port.**
8. The **hippo** on **campus** is **famous** for having a good **memory.**

All it takes is a little practice.

START A MASTER MEMORY FILE.

Earlier we learned how mental filing works by utilizing a simple set of rhyming cue words to tick off our TTDTs (Things To Do Today) and our shopping items (see page 19).

The file in our minds is structured around the basic premise of any filing system. The file drawer in your home or office is there to help you organize the paperwork that comes across the desk. It's there as a catchall for important information, facts, and ideas. Using the ABCs as index cards, you are able to separate one thing from another in order to retrieve what you want more readily. Without filing things away, much useful information might be lost to you, and without setting up an indexing system, much of what you put in the drawer you wouldn't be able to find.

In the simple file system, we created mnemonic connections for the digits from 1 to 10 using rhyming word cues. It's a simple strategy to use when you have a limited number of items to remember. But it has its limitations—it would be impractical to come up with rhyme words for all the digits from 11 to infinity.

The Master Memory File, however, is virtually limitless. Each index tab is labeled with a mnemonic cue that is logically derived from the Numerik Alphabet. Because the system is consistent, it can be extended as far as you can count. As we create index tabs from the alphabet, we set them in the file drawer of our mind.

Begin with the first ten slots, learn the code word for each, and practice with them before expanding the system beyond the number 10.

1 = ha**T**	6 = **SH**oe
2 = ho**N**ey	7 = **C**ow
3 = ho**M**e	8 = hi**V**e
4 = he**R**o	9 = a**P**e
5 = hi**L**l	10 = woo**DS**

The capitalized letters correspond to the sounds in the Numerik Alphabet (see page 30). The other letters in each word are valueless because they are either vowels, W-H-Y letters, or silent letters.

To help lock these code words into your mind until you are more secure with the Numerik Alphabet, make some mnemonic connections to lock each code word in at its respective position.

Code word	Connective thought
1. haT	You can only wear 1 **hat** at a time.
2. hoNey	It takes 2 to make a **honey.**
3. hoMe	Your **home** has 3 bedrooms.
4. heRo	The **hero** is a 4-star general.
5. hiLl	The **hill** is 5 miles high.
6. SHoe	The **shoe** is a size 6.
7. Cow	Get up at 7:00 A.M. to milk the **cow.**
8. hiVe	8 billion bees in the **hive.**
9. aPe	The **ape** is 9 feet tall.
10. wooDS	10 Xmas (X = 10) trees in the **woods.**

Test yourself on the first ten code words to see how well you remember them. If you run into difficulty, rethink your thought that connected the word to the proper number. Write the words down out of sequence and test yourself again.

Once you get these first ten code words down pat, you can file any new information you want to remember in your master file in much the same way you used the rhyme word cues to store information in your simple mental file.

FILE AWAY THE PRESIDENTS.

Try using the Master Memory File by indexing in the first ten United States presidents in their proper order. Make a list of them in order, and then create thought connectors to link them with the index code words.

Code #	Word	President	Connector
1.	Hat	Washington	You're **washing** your **hat** in a **ton** of soapsuds.
2.	Honey	Adams	**Adam** and Eve were the first two **honeys** of creation.
3.	Home	Jefferson	The famous presidential **home,** Monticello, belonged to **Jefferson.**
4.	Hero	Madison	The **hero** is **mad** at **his son** (sounds like Madison).
5.	Hill	Monroe	Marilyn **Monroe** is up on the **hill.**
6.	Shoe	Quincy Adams	Quincy **Adams** stepped into his father John's **shoes.**
7.	Cow	Jackson	Jesse **Jackson** is milking the **cow.**
8.	Hive	Van Buren	Put the **hive** in the **van** that has **beer on** it.
9.	Ape	Harrison	Imagine that nine-foot-tall, hairy **ape** with his **hairy son.**
10.	Woods	Tyler	The **tiler** put down a tile walkway through the **woods.**

Look over this presidential list a time or two and impress your connections in your mind.

Now, for practice in using the Master Memory File, try recalling each president's position in the list without reciting them in order. Write the correct president's name on the line to the right.

Number	Code word	President
2.	HONEY	_____
7.	COW	_____
1.	HAT	_____
4.	HERO	_____
3.	HOME	_____
6.	SHOE	_____
10.	WOODS	_____
9.	APE	_____
8.	HIVE	_____
5.	HILL	_____

Once you get the hang of working with the Master Memory File, you should be able to file away whatever information you care to and retrieve it in whatever order you choose.

FILE AWAY LONG LISTS OF NUMBERS.

Using the Master Memory File, you can even lock in lists of long numbers and retrieve them later. For example, if you used equipment parts numbers in your work and wanted to remember the numbers in a particular order, you can file them away in your Master Memory File and pull them out when you need them.

Let's take the list of numbers from pages 32 and 33, where we first learned the Numerik Alphabet, as an example. First you memorized the numbers using the phrases from the Numerik Alphabet. Once you have the phrases memorized, you can file them away in your master file. Here's how to do it.

The numbers were:	*And the phrases to remember them were:*
314325	My Terminal
7327151	Communicate All Day
849845076	For Beverly's Cash
034131485	Summertime Travel
941710950	Protect Us Please
5105984127709208	Let Us All Buy Everything Expensive
1215122047411741	Don't Let Anyone Use Your Credit Card

First, make a connector thought from your index word to the phrase that represents the number.

No.	Index word	Phrase	Connector thought
1	Hat	My Terminal	My hat is on my computer terminal.
2	Honey	Communicate All Day	I'll communicate with my honey.
3	Home	For Beverly's Cash	Beverly's cash is at home.
4	Hero	Summertime Travel	A hero travels in summer.
5	Hill	Protect Us Please	A hill is in front of us to protect us.
6	Shoe	Let Us All Buy Everything Expensive	Let's buy an expensive pair of shoes.
7	Cow	Don't Let Anyone Use Your Credit Card	Hang the credit card around the cow's neck.

Now, when you need to recall any of the numbers, just go into your mental index file and rethink your connector thought to the phrase it translates into. Then translate the phrase back into the number you need to recall.

It will take practice, but you can do it!

USE A MASTER NUMERIK CODE.

You can create additional code words beyond the first ten. By setting up a Master Numerik Code, you will be able to preserve large amounts of information and have it handy for instant recall.

Using the Numerik Alphabet, words can be created for every number from 1 to as high as you care to go. Each code word is derived logically and consistently from the phonetic sounds of the Numerik Alphabet. TIN, for example, which stands for 12, uses the sounds for 1 + 2 (TiN). We use these code words as index tabs in our mental file, and we connect new information to them. Here are 25 code words to start you off.

1. haT	7. Cow	13. TeaM	19. TuB
2. hoNey	8. hiVe	14. TiRe	20. NoSe
3. hoMe	9. aPe	15. hoTeL	21. waND
4. heRo	10. wooDS	16. DiSH	22. NuN
5. hiLl	11. TiDe	17. DoG	23. gNoMe
6. SHoe	12. TiN	18. DoVe	24. New yeaR
			25. NaiL

You can substitute words you like better, as long as they follow the Numerik rules. First, make each code word a strong, concrete noun, one that you can mentally see and relate to. Second, use the exact phonetic sounds from the Numerik Alphabet in the code words you choose. The important thing is to lock your code words in so that they become as automatic as the ABCs.

To practice using the expanded Master Code, why not continue to index in the rest of the presidents? You can find a list of them in an almanac. Here are a few more connector thoughts—but your own personal ideas will give everything greater sticking power.

The 14th president was Pierce.
14. TiRe   Pierce   You can pierce the tire.

The 20th president was Garfield.
20. NoSe   Garfield   Garfield the cat got shot in the nose.

31 TREAT PEOPLE'S NAMES AS INFORMATION.

Forgetting someone's name can be very insulting and embarrassing—especially if they remember yours. If good service is important in your work, forgetting names can be very costly. Like not remembering any other information, not remembering names is merely the result of a lack of focus. You can unexpectedly run into a coworker or acquaintance and get a mental block—you can't bring up the person's name. This happens because you never consciously collected their name in the first place—you never focused on it.

Treat every name you hear as an important piece of information you want to latch onto. When you hear a name, hit the SAVE key by asking yourself, "What does this make me think of?" Look for the Soniks—the relative or phonetic meaning—in names. This will give names life. Paul Newman's last name describes him as a NEW MAN. Maybe Robert drives a RED FORD. Is Marlon's choice perennially BRAND "O"?

By identifying the Sonik sound the name makes, you're calling your mind's attention to the information the name holds. You are using your "mind's ear" and exhibiting mental control over your memory.

Looking for meaning in names is the major step that can lock names in. It takes focus. That's how you hit the SAVE key. That's how you switch your memory from automatic pilot to power control.

DON'T EXPECT NAMES AND FACES TO MATCH.

32

Most people do not look like their names. Does Joe Black have black hair? Does Harry even have hair? Even so, it's important to notice people's faces when we meet new people. That helps us to connect both the face and the name. Make yourself look at the face of the person you are meeting and take notice of his or her general appearance. But don't focus on clothing. It changes daily—faces don't.

People's faces, as well as their bodies, come in small, medium, and large. Face shapes come in three basic styles: square, round, and oval. Make yourself answer which word describes best the person you are meeting. Notice any outstanding facial features—the teeth, skin, nose, eyes, or mouth. Notice the person's hair (facial as well as scalp) and coloring. Not everyone has some outstanding feature to look at; some faces are distinguishable by their particular expressions—smiles or frowns, for example.

Become face-conscious just as you are becoming name-conscious. Even though the woman with the widow's peak probably won't be named Mrs. Peak or Mrs. Widow, merely by noticing the face as you hear the name, you are connecting the two. Your senses of seeing and hearing are reinforcing each other mentally.

MRS. YOUNGMAN   HARRY   MR. FULLER

Mrs. Youngman might be an older woman, Harry might not even have any hair, and Mr. Fuller might actually be thinner.

33   CATEGORIZE NAMES.

As soon as you hear a name—either a first name or a last name—try to categorize it. Give mental monikers to people as you meet them. People's names fall into two divisions: names that give you meaning, and names that you give meaning to. Some names, like Carpenter, Green, or Price, have built-in meaning. They are quick to latch onto—we recognize the meaning merely by hearing the name. These are Soniks. Any name that is the same as or sounds like a dictionary word of any kind—whether noun, verb, adjective, or adverb—is a Sonik. These names can easily be categorized. Here are some categories you might recognize:

THE NAME'S THE SAME (as that of someone you know):
  Carson, Jackie, Reagan, Bill, Leno, Bryant
PLACE NAMES:
  London, Virginia, Hampton, Montgomery, Santiago
NOUN NAMES:
  Fox, Ball, Barry, Nickel, Church
ACTIVE NAMES:
  Boyle, Cook, Pierce, Pat, Kerry
BRAND NAMES:
  Wilson, Campbell, Ross, McDonald, Heinz
OCCUPATIONAL NAMES:
  Singer, Forman, Baker, Butler, Workman
DESCRIPTIVE NAMES:
  Greene, Young, Fuller, Weiss, Bonnie
FICTIONAL NAMES:
  Heidi, Hook, Sawyer, Bond, O'Hara

Not all names are dictionary words. You can categorize those that aren't by improvising a bit from what you hear and creating Sonik substitutes. Categories for these names include:

NAMES THAT SOUND LIKE WORDS:
  Silbermintz (silver mints), Dade (date), Quigley (quickly), Ridgely (richly), Kendle (candle)
RHYMING NAMES:
  Steven (even), Gerrity (charity), Kirk (work), Demirdjian (diversion), Norman (stormin')
NAMES THAT SOUND LIKE PHRASES:
  Gudlauggsen (good luck son), Perloff (pearl off), Schlomofer (slow mover), Gottschalk (got chalk), Iacocca (I like cocoa)
NAMES YOU CAN TRANSLATE:
  Stein (stone), Montagna (mountain), Schwartzkopf (blackhead), Rico (rich), Altman (old man)

> **HINT**
> Practice listening for, thinking about, and categorizing names. After a while you'll have a ready thought for just about every name you hear. You'll be able to drop it in the right category in your mind.

By categorizing a name as soon as we hear it, we are making an instant connection to the mind's ear. It pairs what you hear with a place to put it.

USE IMAGINEERING.

34

A person's face provides a solid visual cue, reminding you that you've seen it before. But seeing the face doesn't give you a verbal reminder of the name. We need to fasten the name to its owner by collecting the face and the name in the same frame.

We accomplish this with a combination of imagination and mental engineering, or "imagineering." How you do this depends on the category in which you've dropped the name. If you're meeting Miss Reagan, imagine her shaking hands with Ronald Reagan. If you're meeting Mr. London, imagine him on a bridge with Big Ben in the background. Imagine Mr. Boyle over a pot of boiling water. Put Mrs. Campbell in front of a bowl of tomato soup.

Once you've put the name into a category, it's easier to imagine a connection between the person and the name. Practice using imagineering whenever you hear a new name. Soon you'll find it easy to fasten the name to its owner.

35 LOOK AT WORDS FOR SPELLING CLUES.

Almost everybody has certain words they have trouble remembering how to spell. You can use mnemonic connectors to remember how to spell problem words. If you rely on the eyes alone and don't get the mind involved, you could forget the correct spelling of a word by the time you close the dictionary.

The two most important rules to lock in problem words are:

1. Be sure you understand the word's meaning.

2. Tie the meaning to the spelling by noticing spelling clues.

It's easy to remember that there are two *l*s in *balloon* if you notice the *ball* in it. After all, what is a balloon but a round soft ball?

Many people have trouble correctly spelling the word *occasion.* Does it have two *c*s and one *s*, or the other way around? An occasion is an event—make it a Spanish event where CC Señor will remind you of the two *c*s and the one *s*.

Concentrate only on the problem area of the word, such as the final *ar* at the end of the word *grammar.* Think, "Don't MAR your grammar," and you'll solve that problem.

Here are a few more examples:

Make an a**comm**odation for two **c**hildren and two **m**ommies.

Be independ**ent**, and no one can put a **dent** in you.

Expen**$**e always involves **$**.

Mne**m**onic is about **m**ind and **m**emory.

Knowl**edge** gives you an **edge.**

You'll find that the words you consciously connect with by finding their mnemonic clues will be the ones that never give you trouble.

CONNECT THE MEANING WITH THE SOUND.

36

Merely looking up a word in the dictionary is no guarantee you'll remember the definition. The dictionary gives you the facts but doesn't tell you how to remember them. Whenever you take the time to look up a word, take the additional moment to CONNECT the meaning with the sound.

For instance, the word *sarcophagus* means "a stone coffin." The word breaks up into the phonetic sounds of SAR, COFFA, and GUS. To remember a sarcophagus is a stone coffin, just think the Sonik phrase "Sorry you're in the coffin, Gus!"

The term *bel canto* refers to a smooth, sweet style of singing. Just think, "BELLE CAN TOtally thrill us with her sweet singing," and the meaning will be captured for you.

To remember that a *myopic* person is nearsighted, think of "MY OPtIC nerves."

Did you ever hear the word *oxymoron*? If not, this word would be as meaningless to you as a long number you saw for the first time. The first thing to do is find a meaning for it by looking up its definition. The dictionary says that an oxymoron is a phrase created by contradictory terms, such as *deafening silence* or *cruel kindness*. We can use the etymology (derivation) of a word to help us connect with the meaning. In the dictionary it tells us *oxy* means sharp. By recognizing that to be sharp is contradictory to being a moron, you can easily recall the meaning. Knowing the derivation or origin of words is a great help toward building vocabulary.

Sometimes you can use a rhyme in your mnemonic. For the word *penurious,* which means "stingy," you could use the rhyming connector phrase "I'm furious because he's PENURIOUS and won't give me a PENny.

Next time you want to learn a new word, hit your SAVE key by asking yourself what other word or phrase sounds like the new one. Then connect the similar sound cue—the Sonik—with the meaning of the new word. Then start including the word in your conversation and thinking. Eventually the new word will become part of your accessible and permanent vocabulary.

37 CREATE MENTAL HOOKS FOR FOREIGN WORDS AND PHRASES.

The same rules for learning new English words apply to learning words and phrases in foreign languages. Theoretically, it makes no difference whether the word you hear for the first time is a foreign word or an English word. Either one is a meaningless sequence of letters until you furnish the right cues and connections. Make sure you know the correct meaning and pronunciation of the word before you lock in your connection.

Many words are similar in several languages. These are called cognates. And if you're focused, you'll notice the similarities the first time you see or hear them. These similarities will form the mental hooks that will help you remember the words.

Other foreign words have English meanings closely related to similar English words. Here are a few in Spanish:

English	Spanish	Connection
remember	recordar	record
think	pensar	pensive
finish	terminar	terminate
meeting	asamblea	assembly
busy	ocupado	occupied
write	escribir	scribble

Using wordplay, puns, and Soniks, we can work out some mnemonic connections to these greetings from around the world:

Country	Greeting	Sounds like
Japan	Ohayo	Ohio
Korea	Annyong hasimnikka	On your horse, amigo
France	Bonjour	Bon/ny jour/ney
Germany	Guten Tag	Couldn't talk
Denmark	Goddag	Good dog
Russia	Dobriy dye	Do bridge in
Turkey	Gunaydin	Gunga Din

and these "goodbye" phrases:

Country	Parting	Sounds like
China	Tsaijian	Sergeant
France	Au revoir	Oh, river
Germany	Auf Wiedersehen	I'll feed her, Zane
Holland	Totziens	Taught sins
Russia	Dosvidaniya	Those fit on ya
Poland	Do widzenia	Do vat's in ya
Greece	Cherete	Charity

"Do itashi mashite!"

American servicemen stationed in Japan after World War II heard the Japanese phrase for "you're welcome" ("do itashi mashite") and Sonikally coined the phrase "Don't touch the mustache!"

38

PUT FILM IN YOUR MENTAL CAMERA.

Absentmindedness visits all of us from time to time. It has nothing whatsoever to do with intelligence or age. The CEOs of the Fortune 500 companies can be just as apt to misplace their car keys as the junior high school student is to forget his bus pass. We have days when we forget extremely important things and simply can't understand why.

Absentmindedness is a literal term—the mind is absent from the action. And if your mind is absent, you are not thinking about what you are doing. You have no focus, no original awareness. Your eye may be looking, but it is not seeing—like a photographer snapping pictures all day only to discover later that no film was in his camera.

Switch on your conscious mind. Put some film in your mental camera. If you want something to register, think about what you're doing at the moment you're doing it.

39

PREVENT FORGOT-WHAT-I-CAME-HERE-FOR SITUATIONS.

How many times have you walked down the hall to a coworker's office, or gone to the kitchen at home, and when you got there, you didn't know why you'd gone? That's perfectly normal. You can lose a thought as fast as you can get one. To avoid losing it, you must lock it in during the moment of the thought. If you don't, then be prepared to stare into space wondering why you're where you are.

Thinking of going to the garage for a hammer? When you first get the idea, see yourself getting down the hammer from its shelf and perhaps even pounding in a few nails for good visual measure.

Avoid forgot-what-I-came-here-for situations by using your mind's eye. Visualize yourself having already achieved what you are going for—before you even go.

SNAP A MENTAL PICTURE OF YOUR CAR KEYS.

40

Forgetting where you put the car keys is one of the most common results of absentmindedness. The next time you put your car keys down, don't let it be just another unconscious action. Take an instant to snap a mental picture of the keys just where you put them.

If you drop the keys on the kitchen table, don't just drop them off and walk away. Take an instant to picture the keys on the table in your mind's eye. When you do walk away, be sure you can still SEE the keys on that table even though your back is turned.

For further mental insurance, you might add to your picture any other detail on that table—perhaps a bowl of fruit or a decorative piece of pottery. This related detail in your visual picture will make a greater impression on your memory. To add an audio cue to your mental scene, you might replay in your mind the sound the keys made as you tossed them.

One helpful trick is to pick a permanent resting place for your keys: the table in the hall, the top of the TV. Once you've picked an appropriate place, make it memorable by taking that mental picture. Make sure you never put your keys anywhere else.

The same trick can help you find your glasses, your wallet, the book you're reading—anything you tend to lay down automatically. Get in the habit of taking a mental picture whenever you put anything down. Your mind will always be glad to develop it for you.

41 LOCK IN WHERE YOU PARKED YOUR CAR.

How many times have you had the good luck to find a parking space, patted yourself on the back, parked the car, and left—only to return and think it was stolen because you had no idea where you parked it.

For remembering where you parked your car, you need film in your mental camera. Snap a mental picture of the surrounding area and any landmarks. Write yourself a mental memo spelling out just where you are parked, giving yourself a descriptive cue reminder.

Your mental memo might be a rhyme:

"I parked today by May's Cafe."

Or,

"I'll find my car near the Chestnut Bar."

Check the names of the cross streets and make a mental thought connection between them. If you're near Third and Oak, try this mental memo: "Three oak trees." Near Washington and First, remind yourself that Washington was the first president.

Search for the Sonik meanings of the names of the streets, just as you would a person's name. Stanley Street might remind you of your friend Stanley. Ohio Avenue reminds you of the state. Harcourt Avenue sounds like a hard court. Beverly Boulevard might remind you of Beverly Hills, California.

Remembering your car's location at the mall or in a multistoried parking garage poses a special problem. Try to create a mnemonic connector between the general location and the aisle or between the aisle number and color code. If you're parked in the south section, area 4, you might think of the word FORSOOTH. If you're parked in aisle B at the blue level, "Don't B Blue." At aisle D, the purple level, the song title "Deep Purple" can be a good cue. Take a moment to make things easy to remember, and you'll remember them.

LOCK IN THAT GREAT IDEA YOU JUST HAD.

42

Ideas are fleeting—they can be gone in a moment. We have to switch on our conscious and take control of storing them.

To lock in ideas, try to make a mental connection between the idea and a related image or thought. Suppose you and a coworker are hashing over a problem, and it occurred to you that George Schardt was the person to call to help. At the moment his name comes to your mind, lock it in instantly with the image of his face and the thought, "Be smart and call Schardt." Then, at the appropriate time—even minutes later—you'll have a cue to remind you of the name and your idea to call him.

Say a newspaper ad reminds you that the 11th is the last day to enter a contest you have an interest in. See yourself being lucky on the 11th by making a mental memo of 7-11. The 7 represents the lucky number 7, and 11 is the due date. You'll have a better chance of getting your entry in on time.

On the way home from work, you hear on the car radio an exciting offer for a trip to the Greek isles. Although you missed the particulars, you decide to call the station when you get home. That's the moment to lock in the station call letters with any mental connector cue that comes to mind.

If the station is KISS radio in Los Angeles, picture yourself kissing a Greek statue. For WTAX in Springfield, Illinois, imagine paying your taxes with Greek drachmas. For WOC in Davenport, Iowa, use an acrostic phrase: "Why Of Course" (I'd like to go to Greece). By taking a conscious moment to make a mental image from the idea to the call letters, you can remember not only to make the call, but why.

43 BREAK YOUR SPEECH INTO PARTS.

The greatest fear most people have is the fear of speaking before a group. This amazing statistic has shown up in survey after survey. Fear of giving a speech ranks higher on the human fear list than even death. But it needn't be so.

Stage fright is simply the fear of forgetting. The solution is simply to remember what you want to say. Know your subject thoroughly and realize that making a speech involves preparation and organization.

The best way to get prepared is to first decide what points you want to include in your presentation. Then break your speech into parts and write out each part, letting your mind play with the key ideas and examples. Relate the points in your speech to your own knowledge, and personalize it by linking what you want to say with your own experiences.

Before you start to write out your final presentation, you need to set some careful objectives in your mind.

Know:

WHAT your message is;

WHY it is important;

WHERE you're going with it; and

HOW to get there best.

If you keep these objectives in mind, you'll be able to prepare your speech thoroughly. And with thorough preparation, you will know your speech so well that you won't feel like cowering behind the podium.

FILE THE PARTS MNEMONICALLY.

44

Once you have your speech written out, you can file each point in your mind using any of the mnemonic techniques in this book. Organizing your material with mnemonic cues creates a mental outline to keep you on track. The cues act as built-in prompters to remind you of the major points while you are delivering the speech.

Look at the key ideas in each section and select a buzzword or phrase for each point. Now, use the initial letter of each buzzword or phrase to create either an acronym or an acrostic. If the points must be delivered in a certain order, be sure to reflect that order in the acronym or acrostic.

Suppose you were going to make a presentation recommending a site for your organization's convention next year. You want to emphasize the number of hotel rooms available, the number of meeting rooms available, how convenient the site is to a major airport, the presence of good public transportation, and the opportunities for fine dining and nightlife. You could make a list of buzzwords for each point:

Hotel rooms

Meeting rooms

Transportation (public)

Airport

Nightlife

To make sure you remembered these points in order, you could create this acrostic sentence: How Many Tours Are Needed.

You can also file the words in your Master Memory File. Form a connection between each buzzword or phrase and the appropriate index cue. It's possible to combine mnemonic techniques. Perhaps use an acronym or acrostic to lock in the main sections and follow through by filing each point in your master file.

If you've organized your speech with mnemonic cues, you won't need to refer to notes while giving it. In fact, you can leave your notes at home.

45 ASK YOURSELF QUESTIONS AND ANSWER THEM EXTEMPORANEOUSLY.

Do not memorize your speech word for word. This would invite fear of forgetting, since you would have to give it back word for word. Your thoughts would not flow naturally. Memorizing your speech by rote doesn't allow you to digest it with your mind and feelings. You must become totally familiar with your material and relate to it conversationally. Practice by asking yourself questions about each point and then answering them extemporaneously. Understand and believe in the ideas you're expressing. Identify with them. Your speech should be a part of your personal knowledge and self.

Don't rehearse your speech too near delivery time. You'll be under too much tension as the hour draws near; last-minute run-throughs tend to create mental blocks that can repeat themselves at the same spot during your delivery. The best time to practice is when you wake up in the morning—never when you're already on the dais.

Fear of forgetting should be forgotten. When you're on the dais, keep this in mind:

If you treat your presentation like a conversation with the audience—sharing from your heart, not reciting word for word—you'll never have nervous knees. Who ever heard of having stage fright while talking to a friend?

PRACTICE THE NUMERIK ALPHABET BY TRANSLATING YOUR FAVORITE POEM INTO DIGITS.

46

It's always a good practice to keep your machine well oiled. Memory is a wonderful tool. With use it becomes sharper and sharper. It cannot be worn out or used up. Exercise your memory to perfect some of the techniques in this book. To commit the Master Numerik Alphabet to memory, you might practice it by translating a favorite poem into digits. This can be a fruitful and fun way to lock in the Numerik Alphabet.

First write out the entire verse. Next write the appropriate digit over each consonant letter sound, crossing out the vowels, WHY sounds, and silent letters. Then turn the paper over, and sounding out the verse in your mind, try to write down all the correct digits. Once you've done this, check them against the digits on the poem side of the page to see how well you did.

Here's an example:

```
4  0   0   4  4 1
ROSES ARE RED
8  5  10  4  95
VIOLETS ARE BLUE
6  7  4 0 0      1
SUGAR IS SWEET
  21 0     4
AND SO ARE YOU.
```

(The S in SUGAR makes an SH sound.)

47 PRACTICE NUMERIKS WHEN YOU'RE STUCK IN TRAFFIC.

Ease the boredom of a traffic jam by studying license plates. Turn the digits into words or phrases using the Master Numerik Alphabet. This kind of practice will help you to become more adept at using the Master Numerik Alphabet to remember numbers. You'll also probably find it a great stress reliever.

One of the best times to practice on names is when you're comfortably sitting back listening to the late-night news or watching a talk show. You're under no pressure from your daily work or chores, and you're in the privacy of your own domain. And TV provides plenty of names to practice on. Listen for them as they come up, search for their Sonik sounds, and focus on the people they belong to. Once you connect with a name, mentally drop it into a category. When the show is over, see how many you can recall.

You'll find with practice how much easier it is to recollect a name or number when you've connected with it.

With enough practice, you'll find it easy to turn numbers into phrases using the Master Numerik Alphabet.

TURN SHORT-TERM MEMORY INTO LONG-TERM MEMORY.

48

We have no memory of a name, number, idea, or any piece of information before we've heard of it. By collecting the information and connecting with it, we create a short-term memory. The next step is to review our mental connections in order to turn short-term memory into long-term memory.

Reviewing is like rehearsing. The more you rehearse, the better you perform. And reviewing does not mean merely repeating. To review means to bring your original connection back to mind, think about it, and reinforce it. Mindless repetition creates no original thought connection, and no learned knowledge is reinforced.

Review the index words to your Master Memory File, your mnemonic cues, and your connector thoughts when you're physically occupied but your mind is free and available for rehearsal. Fill up your walking or jogging time mentally by going over your index words first and then connecting them with the information you've filed away (such as a list of the presidents or parts numbers). While you're in the shower, run through a list of new names you've categorized. Bring up the thoughts you've used to connect them. This review reinforces your memory and keeps your mind alert.

Organize and learn new information when you're fresh and alert. Save the tired times for review. Right before falling off to sleep is a fine time for reviewing—you're usually in a completely relaxed state, and relaxation is always a good environment for your memory.

On the other hand, if you are having trouble falling asleep, instead of counting sheep, run through your code words, cues, and connectors.

Collect and connect with information to turn it into knowledge. And then rehearse it right into your long-term memory.

49 KEEP YOUR MEMORY HEALTHY.

Memory is a part of your physical and mental self. Just as you would want to keep your body healthy, you should give equal time to keeping your memory healthy. Keep your mind challenged and treat it to good nutrition, plenty of rest, and above all, a positive attitude.

Our memories are often affected by our moods. Even a mild depression can interfere with the mind's ability to absorb information. If you find yourself with negative thoughts, break the chain by seeking some diversion—perhaps going for a walk or to a movie.

If a constant unhappy thought or image seems to perpetuate itself on your mental screen, have a pleasant visual picture ready to pop into your mental camera to replace it. In a click you can banish that nasty neighbor's image with an image of a day at the beach.

To keep a healthy memory as well as a healthy body, follow the rules of good nutrition. Eat a well-balanced diet and avoid excessive alcohol and nicotine—they can be unfriendly to the memory. Drinking alcohol often inhibits the brain's ability to process new intelligence. And for many smokers, breathing in nicotine may also mean inhaling a loss of recall. A number of other drugs also undermine the memory—if you have a question, check with your physician or pharmacist.

Some amount of stress is a regular visitor to most of us in our daily lives. Just enough stress can motivate us to greater performance. Heavy stress, however, can sabotage the memory. Worry and anxiety can clutter your thoughts, leaving little space for learning or remembering. Since mental stress also creates physical tension, the best way to relieve it is through exercise and deep breathing. Exercise should be a regular part of everyone's daily program. Ease your physical tension and your mental stress will be eased as well.

EXPECT TO REMEMBER.

50

This is the end of this book, but it's just the beginning of a whole new habit. Now you know how to take control and push the memory button in order to operate your memory without worry.

Whenever you want to remember new information, you know you can take hold of it by hitting that SAVE key—asking yourself, "What does this make me think of?"

To remember, you must switch on your power and consciously connect the new information with information you already know. Connecting the new to the known makes remembering easier. Trying to recall information without having made those mental connections is like trying to read and write without knowing the ABCs.

You have the formula now to make your memory work for you, and the more you use that formula, the more confidence and personal satisfaction you'll attain. Dispense with mindless repetition that results in the "I forgot" syndrome. Use organized mind-handling and adopt a "yes I can" attitude. Take control of your memory and expect to remember.

Absentmindedness: The condition of being unaware of what is going on.

Acronym: A word formed from the initial letter of each word in a phrase.

Acrostic: A sentence created using words that start with the initial letter of each of the items in a list.

Cognate: A word in one language that is related to a word in another language.

Etymology: The history of the development of a word.

Imagineering: Using the imagination to connect a name to a person.

Long-term memory: The permanent memory of events and information.

Master Numerik Alphabet: A system for remembering numbers by translating them into words.

Master Memory File: A system for memorizing lists using code words derived from the Master Numerik Alphabet.

Memory: The ability to recall what has been learned.

Mnemonics: The science of techniques for memory improvement.

Numeriks: The connection between the sound of a number and what it reminds you of.

Phonetic: Relating to the sounds of speech.

Rote: The attempt to learn through mechanical repetition.

SAVE key: An activity that initiates storing of information so that it can be recalled—such as saying, "What does this make me think of?"

Short-term memory: Memory of very recent events. The number of items that can be put into short-term memory is very limited. For permanent storage, items in short-term memory have to be put into long-term memory.

Soniks: The connection between the sound of a word and what it reminds you of.

A

Absentmindedness, 50–51
Account numbers, how to remember, 32–33
Acronym, 15, 55
Acrostic, 16, 53, 55
Addresses, how to remember, 28–29
Age, effect on memory, 9–10
Anxiety and stress, effect on memory, 6, 60

C

Casals, Pablo, 10
Chanel, Coco, 10
Clemenceau, Georges, 10

E

Ear-mindedness, 23
Eddy, Mary Baker, 10
Edison, Thomas Alva, 10
Exercise, 60

F

Facts and information, how to remember, 34
Focusing, 8, 12, 14, 24, 42, 50, 58, 61
"Focus on People" chart, 11

G

Goethe, 10

H

Health, 60
Hugo, Victor, 10

I

Ideas, how to remember, 53
Illness, 5, 9

J

Kant, Immanuel, 10
Kreisler, Fritz, 10

L

Lists, how to memorize, 19–22, 35–38, 41
Locations, how to remember, 52

M

Master Memory File, 35–40, 55, 59
Master Numerik Alphabet, 27, 30–33, 35–36, 39, 41, 57, 58
Master Numerik Code, 41
Mellon, Andrew, 10
Memory, long-term, 14, 59
Memory, short-term, 14, 59
Mental filing system, 19–20
Mental memo, 18, 52, 53
Mental picture, 20, 51–52
Mnemonics, 13, 14, 15, 19, 35–36, 52, 55, 59
Moods, 60